From My Heart to Yours...
Letters to My Young Sisters

Visit www.booksurge.com to order additional copies.

From My Heart to Yours...

Letters to My Young Sisters

Stephanie Brunner Tillman

Dedicated to Nadren, Nadren Lee,
Lola, and Beverly Jane…
the women who taught me
to know my heart.

Acknowledgments

THIS BOOK IS the result of my genuine desire to speak to the present generation of dynamic, intelligent, and beautiful young African-American women who struggle each day in adolescence and young adulthood. From personal experience, I know that the journey to womanhood is not for the weak or faint of heart, especially in this new millennium. The depth, breadth, and impact of the culture we live in make it very tough for a young woman to navigate the waters of life. I hope this book will provide encouragement to you as you make your way.

To God be the glory for all things. I am blessed and I know it. I am thankful for the presence of God in my life, and for all of the mountains and valleys that I have encountered and will encounter along my journey.

When I reflect on my journey so far, I am grateful for that steadfast assuredness all along the way that my parents loved me, wanted the best for me, expected the best out of me, and demanded the best from me. They set the standard and nurtured me at every turn. Thanks, Mom and Dad. I love you.

To my personal editorial staff, comprised of two of the brightest minds on the planet: Laquan (my sister, mentor, and friend) and Atonya (my "3G"—good, good girlfriend). You girls are the best. Thanks for not holding back!

To my husband, Ben, thank you for your support and encouragement every step of the way. You are truly my life mate and best friend. I love you.

To my son, Trey, you are the love of my heart. You keep Mommy on her toes and you make me smile. I wrote this book, in part, because I want your future wife to be a virtuous woman worthy of your love, and for you to be worthy of hers.

And finally, to the three most important young ladies in my life: my daughter, Lindsay, and my twin nieces, Patriece and Shaniece. While you all are in different places in your journey to womanhood, I see so much of myself in each of you. I want so much for you and hope that this book helps to reinforce the many intimate discussions about life, love, self, and God that we have had along the way. You are my greatest challenge and my greatest joy. You are also my hope and inspiration. Without you in my life, this book would never have been written. I love you very much.

My Dearest Young Sisters,

The words and thoughts I attempt to convey to you in this book truly come from my heart. I wish you prosperity, peace, and the realization of all of your dreams. If you ever wonder or have any question in your mind, let me assure you that you are beautiful, intelligent, and worthy of the best that God has to offer. You are a queen and you have the right to live like one. Insist upon only the best for your life—that is, welcome only the best people in your life, set your sights on the best plan to reach your goals, and set only the best and highest standards for yourself. Make choices that are deliberate and right for you. Be a proactive architect of your future. It will be what you make it!

Sincerely,
Stephanie Brunner Tillman

Table of Contents

*And I sought for a man among them that should
make up the hedge and stand
in the gap before me for the land that
I should not destroy it, but I found none.*
— *Ezekiel 22:30 KJV*

Standing in the Gap

I OFTEN REFLECT ON my girlhood with joyful and fond memories. My teen years in particular were always bright with hope and expectation. My biggest concerns at that time lay only in the seemingly weighty issues of what to wear to remain fashionable at school and which boy I had a crush on. The reality for teens today, however, is different. The pressures to conform to a popular culture which glorifies materialism, self-satisfaction, and nonconformity must be overwhelming. Constantly in search of more "bling," doing what feels good, saying what you want to say, and living without constraints must be absolutely overwhelming. It requires, I think, a measure of personal stamina and free-spiritedness that goes against the grain of our innate humanness and is contrary to that which our very souls crave. As humans, we crave boundaries, structure, and order. But we live in a world that seems to reward and exalt the most outrageous and unrestrained lifestyles and behavior. I am saddened at this state of affairs for many young black women whose teen years are shortened prematurely and unnecessarily. Those who, from their very earliest years, either knowingly or unknowingly, trade in the bright anticipation and light of youth to live on the fringes, seeking a sense of belonging and love through sex, seeking pleasure and escape through drugs and alcohol, seeking beauty through the shortest and tightest clothing, seeking popularity and respect by conducting themselves loudly and boisterously, and neglecting to genuinely seek to develop their minds, bodies, and spirits. The folly of youth is lost and is replaced by hard living very early on in life.

It is to and for young ladies who seek advice and encouragement along this complex journey called womanhood that I write this book. My desire is to attempt to stand in the gap for you and your generation through prayer for your healing and restoration to God. Also, I hope to provide a kernel of wisdom here or there which will encourage you and help to propel you forward despite the many challenges that lie ahead. These letters come from my heart to yours.

To bring Vashti the queen before the king with
the crown royal, to show the people and the princes
her beauty; for she was fair to look on.
— Esther 1:11 KJV

Beauty

VERY LITTLE GIRL wants to be beautiful. From our earliest days, we spend time admiring ourselves in the mirror, we play dress up and we dabble in our mother's makeup. We all learned early on that beauty can be obtained if we assemble the right outfit to compliment our curves, the right makeup to accentuate our facial features, and the right hairdo to top it all off. External aesthetics dictate how beautiful we are.

Unfortunately, the external focus on beauty total disregards the heart. Not the beating heart that pumps blood throughout the body, but the heart of the mind. It is the lifeline from which flows the issues of life. It governs our thoughts and, equally important, our behavior.
There is no beauty without a beautiful heart. Our men-

tal, emotional, and spiritual stability rest upon the foundation of a heart that is genuine, balanced, and seeks no harm to others. There is no hatred, no cruelty, no spite, no strife, no violence, no ill will, and no discord in beauty. Beauty is peaceful and peace-loving; it is a free and cheerful giver. Beauty demonstrates a gentle spirit, a kind heart, and a noble disposition.

My young sisters, I urge you to look beyond the exterior window dressing to find real beauty inside yourselves. Reject our popular culture's standards of beauty which seem to dictate tight and revealing attire, expertly applied makeup, and perfectly styled hair. There is so much more to you than that. Your beauty lies in your giving nature—that internal compass which makes you predisposed to helping and nurturing others. Your beauty lies in your natural consensus-building spirit and your aversion to violence and violent behavior. Your beauty lies in your character and integrity; in your ability to do what's right even if doing what's right is not what is popular.

Your beauty is a virtue. Nurture it. Protect it. Develop it. Realize that its source springs up inside your heart, and let it guide you. A life filled with beauty is one that enjoys the best that God has to offer.

Be not deceived:
evil companionship ruins good morals.
— I Corinthians 15:33 asv

My Crew

IN THE FALL of 1992, I entered law school at the University of Georgia, and I was scared. As confident as I was having graduated just a few months prior with a bachelor's degree in education, I felt so out of my league. There were students in my law class who were seeking to become second-, third-, and even fourth-generation lawyers in their respective families. The practice of law would be second nature to them; it was all they knew. Or so I thought. Much like me having been the daughter of two educators, the teaching profession was so familiar to me that it was virtually ingrained in my DNA. It was what I was supposed to be—a teacher. But I followed my interest and my heart to the law, a journey that led me to classrooms occupied by others who knew they belonged there. I had no frame of reference, I did not know what to expect, and, for the first time in my life, I really felt alone.

Enter Lee, Krista, Lisa, and Adrienne—my crew. We quickly bonded as friends and became each other's strength. We were family, a sisterhood of young women with similar backgrounds, goals, fears, and challenges. We thought alike, we talked alike, and we acted alike. We valued each other. My girls had my back and I had theirs. I do not believe that I would have been able to make it through law school without my crew.

It wasn't until after I graduated from law school that I fully appreciated what my crew brought to my life and how they helped me through. The subtle—and sometimes not so subtle—pressure we exerted on each other was what kept us going, kept us focused, and kept us from quitting.

I realize that the peer pressure could have been misplaced and had an opposite result. It could have been their influence that led me away from the intense study law school required. It could have led me to the club for the perpetual parties that seemed to always be going on. It could have been the source of my demise. But it wasn't. Why? Because my crew was focused and we worked toward a shared ambition.

Your friends' influence on you is significant in ways you may not even be aware of. The old adage that "birds of a feather flock together" is time-tested wisdom. If you hang around with your crew long enough, you will observe yourself doing what they do, talking the way they talk, dressing the way they dress, and living the way they live. Even if you are not consciously choosing to emulate or assimilate that behavior—you will. That influence will permeate your mind in ways you are not aware of, and before you know it, you are an invisible member of the crew. You will be invisible because you are indistinguishable from the rest of the group.

There are, I believe, two ways to combat this phenomenon. You can attempt to resist it or endeavor to manage it carefully. Resistance entails the constant struggle to live above the influence of others. It is contrary to our nature as women, whose primary instinct is to connect emotionally with others in relationships. In other words, our nature is to find a crew and stick with it. Doing so satisfies our need to belong.

The other alternative, and the one I recommend to you from my heart, is to pick your crew members carefully. Do not just accept anyone into your life and into your circle of influence. Be selective, choosing only those who bring to the friendship table something of value. Choose those who look, think, and act positively.

Avoid negative people, places, and things—they are toxic and destructive. Their mere presence in your crew is like cancer. It may start small and appear to be containable, but it will grow, perhaps slowly and quietly, but it will grow and grow. Eventually, it will consume you completely.

Negativity in your crew is terminable. It can kill your dreams, your potential, even your very life. Remember that those with whom you surround yourself wield enormous power in your life. Be mindful to evaluate and select your friends carefully.

*There are two primary choices in life; to accept
conditions as they exist, or accept the responsibility
for changing them.*
— Denis Waitley

Exercising Your Power to Choose

ICROSOFT WORD IS a wonderful tool for productivity in creating documents, but it is not always the most user-friendly program around. Have you ever tried to alter the spacing in an outline or change the bullet-point formatting in Microsoft Word? For a novice like me, it can be a frustrating endeavor.

An observation of note, however, is that Microsoft Word, like most software applications, is preformatted so that users can get up and running very quickly without the need for much setup work. It utilizes what are called "default settings" to set, for example, the font size and style, and the order and array of icons on the toolbar at the top of the screen. While this may be a useful aid for most users, what is does is substitute its judgment to makes choices for the user. And it does so automatically and makes the same decision for every user, which means it does not take into account each user's specific needs, wants, or desires. It just defaults to those same settings we all know and love, whether you want it to or not.

Many young people live their lives in a similar way, allowing others to make choices for them. I call it living by default. Living by default is the practice of allowing someone else to make choices for you without your express permission to do so and without knowing your wants, needs, or desires. When you live by default, someone else makes the decision for you on how your life will turn out.

I encourage you to be a proactive chooser. Make it your mission to actively engage in the business of making choices for your own life. You are in the best position to know what is best and right for you. Never turn that power over to someone else. When you mindlessly follow the crowd, doing what they do without question, you are living by default. When you are apathetic and you don't care enough to make a choice for yourself, you, by default, empower someone or something to act on your behalf to choose for you. The problem is, the chooser may not know much about you, and is someone who most definitely won't have to live with the consequences of the choices they make for you.

When I figured out that I didn't have to settle for the basic selections that Microsoft made for me, I chose to change the font from Times New Roman to something more pleasing to me. And so it is in life. You always have the power to make choices that suit you best.

Had I lived by default, I probably would have become a teacher. As a child of two educators, each of whom spent their entire professional careers of more than thirty years shaping and molding the minds of young people, it was an automatic notion in my head that a teacher was what I was supposed to be. And in fact, I did head down that road for a while, as I studied and obtained an undergraduate degree in education. But in my heart, my choice was the law. I had to get off the auto track to education and choose the path of law. That choice has resulted in a deeply meaningful, challenging, and enjoyable career. It was the right choice for me.

You have the power to choose every day. You choose your friends, how you will behave, where you will go, and what you will do. I encourage you to deliberately exercise your power of choice in a thoughtful way every day, as each choice you make is an integral piece of the intricate puzzle that is your life.

*Not that which entereth into the mouth defileth the
man; but that which proceedeth out of the mouth,
this defileth the man.*
— Matthew 15:11 KJV

The Wrapper

THINK THAT ONE of God's most beautiful cre-
ations is the Black man. Physically strong,
mentally acute, spiritually focused, possessing
a healthy sense of self-confidence, and deeply appre-
ciative of and respectful to women, he provides lead-
ership in his home and community, and he partners
with his spouse to raise Black children to excel.

So then, where are these men? And why aren't more
Black women enjoying healthy relationships with
this kind of men? I've heard some say that this kind
of Black man does not exist. Others say that he exists,
but there are so few like him that finding one is virtually impossible. I may be naïve, but I disagree on both
counts.

I believe that people rise to the occasion presented to them. To the extent that Black men do not appear to be available, perhaps we as Black women are not requiring them to rise. If we are willing to accept anything from them in our lives, anything is what we will get in return. This is true in all of life's relationships.

If you accept him referring to you, or to any other woman, as a "bitch," "trick," or "ho," you are not requiring him to rise. If you permit him to sneak into your home under cover of darkness for the proverbial "booty call," you are not requiring him to rise. If you send the message to him that jewelry, clothes, and money to get your hair and nails done is all it takes to get you to overlook his bad behavior, you are not requiring him to rise. In fact, each time you permit him to treat you in an unacceptable way, you sink to his level. You become an accomplice to his crimes against you. You have the power to control who you will let into your life and the role each person will play. Refuse to accept young men who do not meet your criteria, and do not lower your standards in order for him to meet the mark.

When I see young men today, with their pants sagging below their bottoms, unkempt hair, grabbing their crotches, and hurling profanities in every other word, I truly wonder if those young men ever had anyone set boundaries in their lives. Did their fathers ever discipline them along the way? Did their mothers ever show them gentleness? When the answer to these questions is no, a young boy grows up to be a man without boundaries. And a man without boundaries is a scary thing. He does not respect authority, himself, or others—and that includes you. A man without boundaries will hit a woman, sell drugs, use drugs, steal, cheat, and do harm to others with no remorse. Without boundaries, he has no conscience to guide him. Without God's intervention, he cannot rise to the occasion.

However, the good ones are those with the potential and ability to rise. You know it because you see it in him. He is respectful to his mother, he complies with authority, and he treats you like a lady. He is not perfect (none of us are), but at least he demonstrates the basic human attributes of kindness and respect. Most importantly, he can distinguish right from wrong, and he acts on this distinction by doing what's right and rejecting that which is wrong. In fact, it is his internal compass that makes him so attractive. His chocolate frame and handsome face are merely part of the wrapper, like on a candy bar. The marketing-savvy executives at candy companies make sure the candy bar wrapper is attractive enough to catch your eye and enticing enough to get you to buy it. But after you do, what really matters is what is inside the wrapper. The candy bar itself is what we savor, not the paper. Be sure to look beyond the chocolate frame and handsome face, because it is what is inside of him—what is revealed by his behavior—that matters most.

But the fruit of the Spirit is love, joy, peace,
longsuffering, gentleness, goodness, faith, meekness,
temperance: against such there is no law.
— Galatians 5:22–23 KJV

Sweet Fruit

S AN AVID spectator of high school sports, I often find myself at the basketball gym or football field. Equally as interesting as the game being played, often, is the cast of characters who assemble to watch. One thing I know for sure is that when a team of boys show up to play, a group of girls is not far behind. This is particularly true during the preteen and teen years, when a young female's fascination with the opposite sex is just beginning to develop. Make no mistake; it is natural and very much a part of the course of life. God created the attraction between the sexes and it persists through life for us all. It is a basic part of being human. It is the management and control of this basic human instinct, however, that sometimes bedevils.

One day, I was headed to the basketball gym to peek in on a pick up game. As I was turning into the gym parking lot, two carloads of teenaged girls turned into the lot ahead of me. Before I could park and get out of my car, two young ladies had gotten out of a red car and were hurling derogatory word-bombs at two young ladies who had gotten out of a green SUV. Words like "bitch," "ho," and a variety of other equally offensive and inflammatory terms were being exchanged. These words rolled off their tongues without hesitation or remorse, and, as you might imagine, the words were a prelude to the terrible fight that followed. It was the most disappointing and disgusting display of behavior among young women that I had ever witnessed. I later found out that the young ladies were fighting about one of the young men practicing inside the gym.

It all goes back to that natural attraction. It was the age-old conflict. One of the girls in the red car and one of the girls in the green SUV claimed to be the girlfriend of one of the basketball players in the gym. This feud had been ongoing for several weeks, and in an effort to settle the matter once and for all, the girls loaded up with their friends in tow to go to the gym and confront the young man about this issue. As it turned out, while both young ladies exclaimed "that's my man," in fact, he wasn't a "man" at all, because he was playing them both.

At one point during the fight, the young man, along with the rest of the basketball team, came outside to see what was going on, and when he learned that the fight was about him, he laughed and said, "Them hoes [*sic*] is crazy." Notwithstanding his massacre of the English language, his statement made crystal clear that 1) he did not care about either of the young ladies engaged in the fight, 2) he found their warped display of devotion to him amusing, 3) he did not value them at all as individuals, and 4) he felt no sense of remorse for having played a part in the whole scenario.

So, I asked myself, "What is wrong with this picture?" Well, it depends on who you ask. The girls involved in the brawl are still mad at each other and blame each other for the fight. In fact, even after the fight broke up, they vowed that it was not over and they planned to finish the fight at the next available opportunity. The young man they were fighting over replied that "they asses is stupid" and "they just trippin'." If you ask me, here's what went wrong.

The problem began with an egregious display of profane behavior and language. One of the most unattractive things in the world is a foulmouthed young woman. She lacks control and demonstrates her ignorance by expressing herself with expletives. It's almost like an infant who comes into the world unable to speak, so cries as a means of communication. It is the same with potty mouths who have not yet mastered enough of the English language to express the depths of emotion inside themselves. They, too, resort to unintelligible banter much like an infant's cry, just to be heard.

This kind of behavior is also reflective of her family and upbringing. She was taught these words and appears to be predisposed to resort to fighting to resolve conflicts. Sadly, she is just doing what she has seen others do, and the only thing she knows to do.

My young sisters, the language you use and how you conduct yourself are the fruit of your tree. It tells the world who you are and how you are. It is a message that defines you. Be very careful to guard against being lumped into the "loud and ignorant" box. In that box, you are marginalized and devalued by those who hear your message. You cannot reach your potential or achieve your dreams that way. Have a deep enough level of respect for yourself that you refuse to resort to fighting to resolve a conflict, and you refuse to act out uncontrollably. Practice governing your emotions, and, perhaps most importantly, be sure you are expending your emotions in a way or because of someone that is truly worth it. Be convinced in your heart that it is the right thing to do before you put your credibility, your aspirations, and your life on the line.

The fight scene could have ended in serious injuries or even death. Luckily, it didn't—this time. The next time, however, is not promised. Having a propensity to curse and fight means having a propensity to live on the edge. If this is your chosen method of dispute resolution, be prepared for the day when it doesn't work out like you think it will and you lose the fight. Your life, both literally and figuratively, is on the line.

*The tragedy in life doesn't lie in not reaching your
goal. The tragedy lies in having no goal to reach.*
— *Benjamin Mays*

Future Plans

HAVE YOU EVER given serious thought to your future? Have you daydreamed about what you want to be? Have you wondered what it takes to get to where you ultimately want to go? Do you have a dream for yourself?

As simple as it may sound, dreaming about your future is a wonderful motivating tool to help guide you along your journey of life. Typically, when you determine the desires of your heart, your mind and body will follow the pursuit of those desires until they are achieved. Your dreams will be the fire that burns in your mind as your plan the next steps for yourself. The earnest pursuit of your dreams will keep you on track and focused. That is why it is important for you to dream.

My dream as a young lady was to attend college and become a lawyer. Along the way, I learned that the devil was in the details of how to make that happen, so I had to work to research what it would take to get where I wanted to be. I knew graduating from high school and then college were key components to my future plans, but the particulars of where to go to college, what to major in, and related details were the subject of my dreams. I considered many options before making a choice. It was a wonderful and exhilarating experience to know that a smorgasbord of options were wide open for my choosing.

I encourage you to dream for yourself and determine the desire of your heart. Then take that desire and let it compel you to work toward your goals until they are achieved. I encourage you also to strongly consider attending college or getting some other postsecondary education or vocational training. Merely stopping after you receive your high school diploma almost guarantees you a lifetime of economic struggle, financial dependence, and poverty. Without an education, your earning capacity is significantly limited. The more education you obtain, the more you can expect to earn over your adult working life. In addition to the lifelong economic benefits of obtaining a college degree and/or vocational training after high school, just the learning experience itself is worth it. It is nothing like anything you have experienced before.

I have been privileged to visit many colleges and universities in the United States, and the one thing they all have in common is their sense of adventure. While each has its own unique campus and culture, they all have a certain mystique about them to the newcomer. Young adults, often with their first taste of freedom, attend classes, forge friendships, struggle to adapt, and ultimately enjoy the college experience. It is one that can be life-changing and one that I wholeheartedly recommend. There is something about living in a twelve-by-twelve dorm room with someone who starts out as a complete stranger to you and over time becomes one of your best friends that develops character. There is something about paying tuition and lab fees and buying books that helps you to focus on the path of academic development. There is something about studying for a big test into the wee hours of the morning that helps one to focus on achieving a goal.

If you have the academic credentials to get into college and are considering whether it is for you, I encourage you to do your research. Troll the Internet and find institutions that have academic programs in the fields in which you have an interest. Consider the extracurricular offerings, such as sororities, fraternities, academic societies, civic groups, athletics, intramural sports, leisure and recreational facilities, and the student government association. Examine colleges that are located in the geographic areas where you want to be. Pay particular attention to the housing offerings, both on campus and off campus. Look closely at the total cost to attend and then devise a plan to handle the expense. Contact the college, inquire about financial aid, talk to alumni and current students, and visit the campus if you can. Make an earnest effort to learn as much as you can about the college and what it will take for you to be admitted as a student. This kind of diligent effort will help you to determine which college is right for you, and will help you to understand the things you will need to make your collegiate dreams come to life.

Once you have decided where you want to go, set your mind to do what you have to do to get there, to pay for it, and to remain there until you graduate. When done right, college not only prepares you for a career, it helps to prepare you for greater citizenship and involvement in your community. It equips you with a set of skills, experiences, and a degree that is yours forever. Don't cheat yourself out of this terrific opportunity.

If you determine that college is not for you, I strongly urge you to seek post-high school training at a technical college, vocational program, or trade school.

These kinds of institutions can prepare you for the job market in a shorter amount of time than college, usually six to twenty-four months. They can give you targeted training in your area of interest, and when you enter the job market you will be positioned to earn pay greater than minimum wage and/or be poised for entrepreneurship.

The bottom line is, whether college or technical training is your choice, have a goal. Aspire to something greater than a high school diploma or a GED. It would be a tragedy for you not to think ahead and plan for your future. Dream your plans and plan your dreams.

Shame may restrain what the law
does not prohibit.
— *Lucius Annaeus Seneca, Roman Philosopher*

No Shame

JERRY SPRINGER AND Maury Povich have done Black folks (and others) a terrible disservice with their talk shows. They paved the way with their over-the-top, in-your-face sensationalism designed to shock us and outrage our senses. Pushing the envelope and crossing the line of decency and responsible journalism, they created shows which expose the ridiculous, the outrageous, and the absurd. Having no redeeming value, these shows facilitate the airing of very private and dirty laundry in a very public and shameless way.

Amazingly, the participants on these shows, many of whom are Black, willingly expose themselves and their families on national television for the world to see. Secrets that should be held closely are openly disclosed, discussed, and debated. And for what?

Entertainment (and I use that word loosely) purposes only. Certainly not to support, encourage, or facilitate the personal progress or rehabilitation of any of the participants. In fact, these shows make their ratings at the expense of the emotions and reputations of those who appear as guests.

The most embarrassing, degrading, and exploitative shows are, I think, the Maury Povich shows dealing with paternity tests, where young women and their many various sex partners consent to be tested to confirm the paternity of a child. Some women test as many as four or five men in search of a paternity match. One young lady tested nine men, with no confirming match. On grand display, she revealed to the world that she was promiscuous and foolish time after time, having unprotected sex with various men. The men are no better, displaying similar promiscuity and making reference to the many children they have fathered by other women. As if the mere fact that multiple paternity tests are necessary in the first place isn't bad enough, the test participants often begin and end their segment of the show with profanity-laced name-calling, extreme emotional outbursts, and seemingly uncontrolled reactions to the paternity test results. Some call it entertaining reality television. I call it a shame. Shows like this encourage the stereotype that young Black people are ignorant, self-destructive, and devoid of ambition, with no greater aspirations than making babies out of wedlock. To avoid playing into this stereotype and adding validity to it, there are just some secrets best not told and some revelations best kept private.

Shows like this have dulled our sensibilities. We have seen so much that now we are no longer shocked or surprised. Shows like this bombard our consciousness so much that this kind of behavior appears commonplace and acceptable. As a result, we don't observe the boundaries of personal dignity anymore. Young people seem far too willing to tell their business in a public forum, demonstrating a lack of modesty and having no shame.

I encourage you to preserve your dignity and protect your reputation by keeping your vulnerabilities and personal business out of the public's view and hearing. Be modest enough to keep some things to yourself.

That which has been is what will be, that which is
done is what will be done and; there is nothing new
under the sun. Is there anything of which one can say,
"Look! This is something new"? It has already been in
ancient times before us.
— Ecclesiastes 1:9–10 NKJV

You Know Better

HAS YOUR MOTHER ever expressed disappointment in your behavior and, in response to something you had done wrong, said, "You know better"? As a mother of two young children, I find myself saying that all the time. What I mean when I say it is that I expect better from my children because they have seen, heard, and been instructed in the past not to do what they are doing. It means they should have a greater awareness and understanding because they are familiar with the issue and the results of their behavior.

Despite knowing better, according to the Council of Chief State School Officers website, each year about three million teenagers will contract a sexually transmitted disease. Approximately 870,000 teenage girls will become pregnant. Popular culture reflects that the drug of choice for young adults today is marijuana. It seems that it is becoming an "acceptable" choice among young people, with very little stigma attached to its use. Designer drugs like Ecstasy and similar mood-enhancing agents are readily accepted by some young folks as a key component of having a good time. Hip-hop culture extols the superiority of alcoholic drinks such as Cristal, Hypnotiq, and Hennessey and declares "ain't nothin' wrong" with smoking a little weed from time to time. The mega-performers on television sell this lifestyle and it seems that young folks accept the sales pitch hook, line and sinker. I scratch my head in confusion about this. I just don't understand it.

How is it that, in the year 2008, there are new cases of STDs among teens? How is it that there are new teen pregnancies today? How is it that there are new drug addicts and new alcoholics? In this day and age, there should be no new STD cases, no new teen pregnancies, no new drug addicts, and no new alcoholics. Why? Because you know better. There is too much information available to you for you not to know. The Internet, public health campaigns, and the news constantly bombard our society with messages of prevention and treatment, as well as inform us of statistics and epidemics. Today's young adults are arguably more sophisticated and better informed than any of the generations that have come before. How could you not know? And if that's not enough, you know because you have seen these things with your own two eyes. They are all around you. You've heard someone talking about the weed they smoked over the weekend. You know of someone who was driving while drunk and had a car wreck. Perhaps you know a young lady at school who is pregnant...again.

It baffles me that these kinds of things keep happening. It is no secret that unprotected sexual relations can result in the transmission of infectious diseases and can result in pregnancy. You know. It is also no secret that drug and alcohol experimentation is the first step toward addiction. You know. So why then do we continue to see new cases of STDs, addiction, and teen pregnancies among young adults?

One reason these phenomena continue to occur is that the young people who engage in such reckless and self-destructive behavior simply don't think it can happen to them. They tell themselves things like "I know what I am doing" or "It's not that big of a deal" or "It's just a little fun" or "I'll take a chance just this one time," never realizing that one time can be all it takes to alter the course of your life forever.

I encourage you to never take chances of any kind with your life and well-being. You may be lucky enough to avoid the worst once or twice, but ultimately your behavior will catch up to you. Bottom line: if you know better, then do better.

Death and life are in the power of the tongue:
and they that love it shall eat the fruit thereof.
— Proverbs 18:21 KJV

Sticks and Stones

WORDS ARE POWERFUL. The ideas they communicate can be life-changing. If a girl grows up constantly being told that she is beautiful, intelligent, and capable, she will believe those words and live like she believes them. She will carry herself in a way that demonstrates her beauty; she will participate in activities that challenge her intellect and reveal her capabilities. At her very core will be a belief in the encouraging words that took root in her mind from her earliest days.

On the other hand, the power of words can work in a negative way. If a girl grows up constantly being told that she is ugly, stupid, and worthless, she will live up to these words. When she mentally accepts that she has no talent or offerings of her own as an individual, in order to live she will resort to survival mode.

Perhaps, having no greater aspirations than to find a man she can manipulate or bargain with to gain material things such as money, jewelry, clothes, and the like; she reveals a certain shallowness about herself. Being so superficial, she unknowingly sacrifices her self-worth and self-esteem in exchange for the hollow and fleeting joy a new hairdo and a new outfit can provide. She sees other Black women through the lens of competition rather than community. She is quick to engage in controversy, with her own speech peppered with degrading and misogynistic words directed toward others who share her pigment, her gender, and her life's plight.

Her concept of sisterhood is warped and distorted, based solely on her narrow view. In many respects, her life's value is bound up tightly in the acceptance or rejection she receives from the "thug" in her life. She is not offended by the characterization of her boyfriend as a thug; in fact, she relishes it. The more thuggish, the better. She seeks out a young man who has been in trouble with the law, who engages in the drug trade, who is constantly strapped with a weapon, and who casually uses drugs. She affectionately calls him "my nigger" and she bathes in the sunlight of his attention. She empowers him to freely flex his thug muscles in the relationship. She accepts his infidelity and lies, and she is complicit in his assault against her psyche. The assault comes not only in the form of physical strikes—the most powerful blows come in the form of his words. To his boys, he refers to her as his "piece" and she is okay with that. His referring to her this way strips her of her womanhood and humanness, but she doesn't seem to mind. The most telling and hurtful verbal assaults, however, occur to her face, when he tells her she is nothing without him, that no one else wants her, that she's unattractive and not very smart.

Words like these wreak havoc on her self-esteem and self-worth because she is so wrapped up in him. Sadly, she does not realize that his awful words are the weapons he uses to control her. He is even able to mask his own personal shortcomings and inadequacies by making her self-conscious about herself. All the while, she is oblivious to the impact his words have on her life.

Words can build dreams or tear down dreamers. They can create works of beauty or destroy the workers. Sticks and stones may break your bones, but words can crush your spirit.

*I am what I am because of the choices I made
yesterday. I will be what I will be tomorrow because
of the choices I make today.*
— Unknown

Choices

LIFE PRESENTS A smorgasbord of choices every day. Imagine an all-you-can-eat country buffet with its array of offerings. You'll find several meat options, vegetables and side dishes galore, breads and rolls, a salad bar, a dessert station, and all kinds of beverages to choose from. As a paying customer, the choice is yours. In a similar way, life presents a wide array of choices every day. Your challenge, however, is to make good choices for yourself. Good choices are those which are useful and necessary for you and the goals you are trying to accomplish.

Making good choices involves a thought process in which you consider critical facts such as your goals, your abilities, your desires, and the impact of your actions (or inaction) on others. There should be a consideration of the moral rightness of your choice, as well as an evaluation of how and whether your choice is consistent with God's plan for your life. With all these considerations, you may wonder: What is the process for making a good choice? What do you do to ensure a good result every time?

Of course, there are no guarantees or magic formulas. Even the most well-thought-out and planned choice may not end up like you want it to. But to guide you in the decision-making process, Suzy Welch—author, businesswoman, and wife of business guru Jack Welch—advocates the 10/10/10 rule. When faced with an important decision, ask yourself what will be the impact of this choice in ten minutes, ten months, and ten years. If you are comfortable that your choice is productive and good in all three time frames, then by all means, go for it. If it meets an immediate short-term need or desire only, and does nothing to support, encourage, or ensure success in the longer term time frames, be wary and cautious. Your choice today holds consequences for the future. Resist the urge to choose short-term pleasure and comfort over long-term progress and achievement. Choose for the long haul, ensuring yourself the foundation you will need to progress and succeed throughout life.

Train up a child in the way he should go and when
he is old, he will not depart from it.
— Proverbs 22:6 KJV

Now What?

IN 2000, AND again in 2002, my life changed dramatically and permanently. My son and daughter made their dynamic entries into my life and I haven't been the same since. At the time of this writing, they are seven years old and five years old, respectively, and they have taught me so much about them and about myself. I learned that my capacity to love is boundless. As a mother, I know this love because of the boundless and unconditional love they give to me. I learned that I need help. As self-sufficient, self-confident, and self-aware as I think I am, I know that I need help, support, and encouragement. As a mother, I know this because my children need help in every facet of their lives and they look to me for the help, support, and encouragement they require. I learned that forgiveness of myself and others is critical if I want to have joy and peace in my life. As many times as I have studied my Bible and heard sermons from the preacher on the necessity of forgiveness, the lesson really hits home as I watch my children forgive themselves, each other, and me, time after time.

The changes my children have brought to my life have made me a better person. No doubt my focus is aligned in a way that it never has been before. My priorities are clear. My children are at the top of my list.

If you are a young mother who just brought a precious new life home from the hospital, you may be wondering: now what? What do I do with this baby? Regardless of the circumstances within which your baby was born—whether you are a teen or young adult, whether you are married or single, whether you are wealthy or poor, whether you feel prepared or unprepared—your obligations to this baby must now be your priority. Hopefully, your maternal instincts will compel you to love your child completely and unconditionally. This means providing a safe and secure home environment, teaching values like kindness, respect, and caring for others, imposing discipline and setting boundaries, and maintaining high expectations for achievement.

So, you ask, now what? Now you are a full-time nurse, caregiver, cook, laundry attendant, teacher, entertainer…mother. While your days and nights will now be consumed with meeting the needs of this dependent new life, your goal and singular focus should be to raise this child in such a way that you put yourself out of a job. In the final analysis, you want a confident, independent child who is able to think for herself and make good choices in life. Ultimately, you want a child who will grow up to be a well-rounded, well-adjusted adult who can take care of herself and maybe even, one day, take care of you.

The dramatic and lasting changes your baby brings to your life can and will make you a better person if you let them. Learn a love deeper than you've ever known before. Forgive and be forgiven time and time again. Help, support, and encourage. The experience of motherhood is what you make it for yourself and your child. Make it the best it can be.

*The definition of insanity is doing the same thing
over and over and expecting different results.*
— *Benjamin Franklin*

Insanity

Y FRIEND'S SON is an incredible athlete. While football is his sport of choice, he is the kind of young man who excels at every athletic undertaking in which he participates. He is a terrific sprinter in track, he is an incredible point guard in basketball, and he is one of the best baseball pitchers I have ever seen. And as great of an athlete as he is, he is just as poor as a student. Academics in the classroom seem to elude him. He is capable, but truthfully he is not very interested in his school work and the effort that it requires to make good grades. As a result, he works just enough to pass his classes so that he can play sports. He has no other motivation.

When I asked him what he plans to do after graduation, he emphatically responded that he planned to go to college on a football scholarship. I saw a sparkle in his eyes and enthusiasm about the notion of going to college that really impressed me. I could tell this was truly his heart's desire. My alma mater, University of Georgia, was where he wanted to go, and I wholeheartedly agreed that it was a wonderful place to have his college experience. I inquired about what he was doing in order to make this dream come true. He said he was playing and practicing hard, and was determined to give his best performance on the field when the collegiate scouts were watching. He was working out with weights to get stronger and bigger and was watching game films every chance he got so that he could improve his game. Again, I was impressed with his zeal and desire.

When I asked whether he had the grades to get in, he indicated that he was passing and thought he would be okay in the grades department. So, I asked whether he had passed the state-mandated high school graduation test and he told me he had not. He said that he had taken it twice and had failed the math and social studies portions of the test both times. Despite this significant obstacle that remained between him and his college dream, he was still very enthusiastic about the prospect of being able to go to college.

As I pondered further, I wondered what his plan was for passing the graduation test so that he could get to where he wanted to be. That's when he dropped the bomb on me. He told me (drum roll, please) that his grand plan was to just keep taking the test until he passed it. "That's it! That's your plan?" I asked. He proudly nodded affirmatively. I, on the other hand, was perplexed. He was confused by my dismay, so I had to break it down for him.

As bright and talented as he was, he could not see that his effort of approaching the test the same way, time after time, and expecting to have a different result didn't make sense. Nowhere in his plan for future test-taking was there the idea to sign up for a graduation test study course, or the intent to get a tutor to assist with test prep, or even the thought to read and study on his own to improve his test performance. His plan, very simply, was to keep going back and taking the test over and over again each time it was offered, in the hope that one day he would luck up and pass the test. Insane. Simply insane. His entire dream of future college attendance and athletics hinged upon this insane plan working. If it failed, he wouldn't be offered a football scholarship, nor would he be going to college at all, because a passing score on the graduation test is required for admission to all accredited colleges and universities in the state of Georgia. This was his grand plan, with so much hanging in the balance, and he didn't even realize why this was a problem.

If your approach to problem-solving is to do the same thing the same way yet expect a different result—that is an insane notion. This kind of thinking leads to failure, disappointment, missed opportunities, and unrealized dreams. I encourage you to ditch the insanity and devise a real plan to reach your goals.

About the Author

*S*TEPHANIE BRUNNER TILLMAN is a native of Thomasville, Georgia. Since 1995, she has worked for a Fortune 500 company, serving in various legal roles and currently as Vice President and Associate General Counsel. Active in her local community, Tillman wrote this book in an effort to spur local youth, especially young ladies, to value themselves, recognize their potential, and strive to achieve their dreams. This is her first book.

Her education includes a Bachelor of Science in Education from the University of Georgia, a Juris Doctor from the University of Georgia School of

Law, and a Master of Business Administration from Thomas University in Thomasville, Georgia.

She is married and has two children.

Made in the USA
San Bernardino, CA
25 March 2014